Top Down Thinking in a Bottom Up World
A CHRISTIAN VIEW OF
IDENTITY, PURPOSE, AND BEHAVIOR

F. Michael Grubbs, DCoun

Copyright © 2017 F. Michael Grubbs

All rights reserved.

Published in conjunction with The Lyndon Center, LLC

For information about permission to reproduce selections from this book email The Lyndon Center at info@thelyndoncenter.com.

Graphic Cover Design by Charissa Burns
charissaburnsstudio@icloud.com
Instagram @charissaburnsstudio

ISBN-13: 978-1-7322017-2-9

DEDICATION

I Dedicate this book to three people who have greatly impacted my life.

Carolyn Grubbs, my mother

Frank D. Grubbs, my father

Carol S. Grubbs, my wife and best beloved.

F. Michael Grubbs

FOREWARD

I had a preconceived idea of what this book would be about before I began reading it. I could not have been more wrong.

Top Down Thinking is like a sweet Vidalia onion. As you peel away each layer of Mike Grubbs' insight, the fragrance of God's truth hits you like a velvet-covered brick.

I quickly related to the idea of being a bottom-up thinker because I am a frail human, unable to truly understand who I am in Christ, cannot fathom how much He loves me, and am often afraid to embrace the plan He has for my life.

Top Down Thinking plows through those faulty thought processes and compels the reader to think in a new way that, when embraced, will revolutionize the way we live each day.

Top Down Thinking leads the reader to realize that their identity is found in Christ alone ... alone! When we begin to catch a glimpse of how God sees us and understand how deeply He loves us, we begin to evolve into a Top Down Thinker.

Top Down Thinking helps the reader capture the truth that God has a purpose for our life. We are significant. We matter because we were created in response to God's plan – not as an afterthought. When God transforms us from bottom-up thinkers to top-down thinkers, that unique plan God has for us unfolds before us.

Top Down Thinking enables the reader to celebrate the freedom God intends for us and how that liberty changes our behavior. God frees us from our old way of life, but he also frees us to believe and wholly trust him.

I can honestly say that this book will change your life when you employ the truths Mike has so beautifully unearthed and explained in a way we can easily understand and apply. It is an honor to wholeheartedly endorse *Top Down Thinking*.

Mary Southerland

• • •

Mary Southerland, author of *Sandpaper People* and *Hope in the Midst of Depression* (and 6 more books), is an internationally popular speaker at women's retreats and conferences as well as events for women in ministry. She is also a cofounder of Girlfriends in God, a nondenominational conference ministry. Mary lives in Kansas City with her husband, Dan, who is founder of The Movement Group (A Church Planting Ministry). They have two children and six grandchildren.

TABLE OF CONTENTS

Introduction ix

Part One Identity:
It Is All In The Words 1

Chapter 1 The Old You, The New You 3

Chapter 2 Out Of The Heart The Mouth Speaks ... 13

Chapter 3 Language Is The Diagnostic Indicator .. 23

Part Two
Purpose: Change The Words, Change The Mind 33

Chapter 4 The Attitude Of Jesus 35

Chapter 5 God's Will For You (Generic) 41

Chapter 6 God's Will For You (Specific) 49

Part Three Behavior:
Living Top-Down In A Bottom-Up World 61

Chapter 7 Freed From Shackles 63

Chapter 8 Worry-Less 73

Chapter 9 Confidence: Strong And Courageous 81

BIBLICAL REFERENCE LIST

Versions are so noted with each reference used.

ESV   The Holy Bible: English Standard Version (Wheaton: Standard Bible Society, 2016).

NIV   The Holy Bible, New International Version. (Grand Rapids: Zondervan Publishing House, 1984).

NLT   Tyndale House Publishers, Holy Bible: New Living Translation (Carol Stream, IL: Tyndale House Publishers, 2013)

TNIV   The Holy Bible: Today's New International Version. (Grand Rapids, MI: Zondervan, 2005).

INTRODUCTION

I undertook this project because I have reviewed nearly four decades of client files for another project on which I am working. I rediscovered two frequent questions that nearly all clients have asked; "Who am I?" and "What am I to be doing?" These are foundational questions. A fulfilled life depends on how these questions are answered. Wrong answers lead to an ever deeper and more convoluted mess! Only the right answer leads to an abundant life.

We tend to see ourselves as we think we are. We call it identity. This identity is formed by others giving us feedback, even from our earliest memories. As our identities are formed we begin to see ourselves as needing improvement. For example, "be more considerate..." "you are not the center of the universe..." "share with your brother (implying your brother is as important as you are, but how could that be)?" Well-meaning parents, Sunday school teachers, school teachers, peers, etc. are always correcting and setting standards of behavior. We begin by seeing ourselves as two people: one, the center of everything and perfect; two, the deficient one, always needing improvement. As time goes by, we are given more and more feedback by others. A few of us will maintain our self-centered "I'm nearly perfect" identity. The vast majority will find their identity in "deficiency," always needing improvement, always not quite enough. Of this vast majority, there will be two types. Some will try to overcome this deficiency, some will submit to it. The long-term outcomes should be evident. The overcoming types become strivers, but ever unhappy because they can never reach the goal of perfection. The submitters will settle for being the best failures they can be, but failures nonetheless. Identity is so important that we can never just ignore it. I call this bottom-up thinking. That is the premise of this book.

The Gospel (Gospel means good news) teaches something quite different. Simply, it teaches us that we are made as we are, by genetics and environment, shaped by God into the person he wants us to be over a lifetime of person to person relationship with him. By God's design he loves us, chooses us, adopts us, and begins to make us into the unique (one-of-a-kind) likeness of Jesus he means for us to be. No two of us will be like Jesus in the same way because of this uniqueness, yet we will be like him. This is communicated in many ways and places throughout the New Testament but here succinctly:

> *It is God's will that you should be sanctified:* **(1 Thessalonians 4:3a,** TNIV).

Sanctified means 'made holy'. God always accomplishes his will. This is what it means to be God! Well, if God means to make me holy, I shall be made holy. God cannot fail; therefore, I have hope. With this view, I can see from the top down. My inadequacies, my lack, my failure, the areas in which I must be improved do not doom me because God knows about them and is in the process of making me holy.

> *And I am sure of this, that he who began a good work in you will bring it to completion at the day of Jesus Christ* **(Philippians 1:6,** ESV).

What God begins, he finishes. This top-down thinking fills us with hope, gives us <u>holy identity</u>, <u>holy purpose</u>, and encourages <u>holy behavior</u>.

This book is broken into three parts. Part One is concerned with top-down thinking regarding identity. Part Two is concerned with top-down thinking regarding purpose. Part Three deals with top-down thinking regarding our behavior. All three parts will show the faulty ways of bottom-up thinking that our broken world teaches us and the glorious freedom of thinking from God's perspective, the God who is preparing us to live in his magnificent presence forever.

PART ONE
IDENTITY: IT IS ALL IN THE WORDS

F. Michael Grubbs

CHAPTER 1
THE OLD YOU, THE NEW YOU

It is assumed that all cultures and all societies in the world teach a "bottom-up" way of thinking. This means that, as human beings, we approach every situation or circumstance from an anthrocentric (man centered) attitude or posture. We begin thinking from a "me" or "I" point of view. At best, we may be taught to be considerate of others, to sometimes see "through their eyes," to walk a mile in their shoes, etc. But even so, it begins with man and approaches God from this bottom-up perspective.

This man-centered thinking is understandable in those who do not have faith in Christ, those who claim no new birth.

> *In reply Jesus declared, "I tell you the truth, no one can see the kingdom of God unless he is born again"* **(John 3:3,** TNIV**).**

The word "see" in Greek is: εἴδω ĕidō, i'-do; a primary verb; used only in certain past tenses to know:—be aware, behold, consider, (have) know (-ledge), look (on), perceive[1], Therefore, what Jesus is telling Nicodemus in this passage is that one must be reborn, made alive. Paul says something similar in his letter to the Ephesians:

> *But because of his great love for us, God, who is rich in*

> mercy, ⁵*made us alive with Christ even when we were dead in transgressions—it is by grace you have been saved* **(Ephesians 2:4-5,** TNIV).

We must be born of the Spirit.

> *Jesus replied, "I assure you, no one can enter the Kingdom of God without being born of water and the Spirit.* ⁶ *Humans can reproduce only human life, but the Holy Spirit gives birth to spiritual life* **(John 3:5-6,** NLT).

One cannot perceive the Kingdom of God, the "spiritual realm," unless they are raised from spiritual death which is the result of sin. The reason for this is that there is no awareness of the spiritual realm! The spiritually dead dwell entirely in the realm of the five senses; seeing, hearing, tasting, smelling, and touching. When one's spirit is raised from the dead (born again) he/she is keenly aware of the spiritual realm, a sixth sense is added! The incarnation of the "Word" of God, Immanuel (means God with us), is then extremely important because the Spirit of God came to sow the holy seed (spiritual) into the virgin girl, Mary (human), producing the entrance of God into humanity. Thus, the spiritual realm and the realm of the five senses were joined in the person of Jesus Christ and those who believe in him.

> *For those God foreknew he also predestined to be conformed to the image of his Son, that he might be the firstborn among many brothers and sisters* **(Romans 8:29.** TNIV).

Jesus, by his Spirit, led the way for us to participate in the same union of the spiritual realm and the realm of the five senses. This enables us to see from the perspective that God enjoys. When he looks at you (his eye is never turned from you) what does he see? When you look at yourself from the bottom-up what do you see? It is NOT the same thing!

Two aspects of bottom-up thinking are: perceiving ourselves as having only faults, or having no faults. It is most likely that one would have a combination of both, but one aspect would prevail over the other. For example, a person might say: "I'm not a bad person, I never killed anyone;" while thinking that "I have never measured up to my potential, my failures outweigh my successes, I need to improve in so many areas I don't even know where to start." Or, one might say, "I'm a good person. I treat everyone fairly, I pay my bills and taxes, I am generally liked," etc. This person forgets the harsh words, the inconsideration, the opinionated behavior, the lack of compassion, anger, rage, bitterness, resentment, prejudice, etc. that has characterized his/her life in the whole or partially. This is bottom-up thinking. In either of these ways of thinking we are only seeing through our own eyes, the eyes of others, or the eyes of society or culture. Bottom-up thinking is particularly destructive and gives a false identity. Sometimes this false identity is too high, meaning arrogant or conceited; more often it is too low, worthless, hopeless, never good enough. Either way, it is always false.

> *So I tell you this, and insist on it in the Lord, that you must no longer live as the Gentiles do, in the futility of their thinking. [18]They are darkened in their understanding and separated from the life of God because of the ignorance that is in them due to the hardening of their hearts. [19]Having lost all sensitivity, they have given themselves over to sensuality so as to indulge in every kind of impurity, and they are full of greed* **(Ephesians 4:17-19, TNIV).**

Gentiles (those without faith in Jesus) live in futility, producing no useful result. They are purposeless and fruitless regarding eternal things. This is the way they think; "in futility." Their understanding (how they think) is darkened and separated from the LIFE OF GOD due to the hardness of their hearts toward God. This makes them ignorant of God and who he is! They have no sensitivity to the spiritual realm and participate only in sensuality (the five senses). This produces every kind of impurity and greed. All from BOTTOM-UP THINKING!

If you are satisfied with this perspective, this view of yourself (bottom-up thinking), you should stop reading this book immediately! It is not my intention to disrupt your peace. My suspicion, however, is that your peace is already disrupted and you are seeking, perhaps desperately seeking, true, real, and lasting peace. If this is so, read on.

I am glad you made the decision to continue. From this point on, it is assumed that you are seeking another way to navigate this world and into the next. We will begin with identity. Webster defines identity in the second part regarding individuals as:

a: the distinguishing character or personality of an individual: INDIVIDUALITY
b: the relation established by psychological identification[2]

The foremost identifier of you is you! Think about that sentence. How do you "see," perceive yourself? When the only way you can see yourself is by the reactions of others in social context, by the way others speak to you and describe you, by the way you perceive your place in the world; this is bottom-up thinking. It is most likely the only way you have been able to discover who you are, UNTIL NOW! God has made you to be unique, one-of-a-kind. There is only one of you and there will never be another. God views this as very precious to him. He has determined that he wants you in his family.

> *Even before he made the world, God loved us and chose us in Christ to be holy and without fault in his eyes.* [5] *God decided in advance to adopt us into his own family by bringing us to himself through Jesus Christ. This is what he wanted to do, and it gave him great pleasure* **(Ephesians 1:4-5,** NLT).

Notice, Paul says God loved us before he made the world. You have never NOT been loved. Then God says that the reason he chose you is so that you would be holy and blameless, without fault. How can that be? We are all with much fault, you might say. True, but for the words "in Christ." Jesus died taking your sin away from you, all of it! Past, present, and future sin is paid for by the matchless blood of the Savior, Jesus. This does not give us a "free pass" to sin, instead it makes us desire to serve and please him more and more. Furthermore, verse 5 says that God has adopted you into his family by bringing you back to himself by the sacrifice of Jesus on the cross; the debt-paying blood he shed for you. As if that were not enough, which it surely is, it was God's will to do this, he wanted to do it! And it gave him great pleasure to do it! **He is pleased to have you in his family!** This is your identity if you trust Jesus with your life. You are a chosen, adopted, holy member of God's family and he is well-pleased. If you are having difficulty with this please re-read **Ephesians 1:4-5** above, meditate on it, pray and ask the Holy Spirit to give you understanding, and let the truth sink deep inside your soul, and it is plenty good to weep for joy!

How do we make this real for us, here on earth, now? What is our part in receiving all this goodness from God? Well, to receive all the goodness from God, all we need do is consider the verse prior to verses 4-5 above.

> *All praise to God, the Father of our Lord Jesus Christ, who has blessed us with every spiritual blessing in the heavenly realms because we are united with Christ* **(Ephesians 1:3,** NLT**)**.

First, notice what we are blessed with, EVERY SPIRITUAL BLESSING IN THE HEAVENLY REALMS; then notice the tense. He has already done it! Who is it for? Everyone united with Christ. Everyone who believes and trusts in him!

> *And without faith it is impossible to please God, because anyone who comes to him must believe that he exists and that he rewards those who earnestly seek him* **(Hebrews 11:6,** TNIV**)**.

Simply and profoundly believe. Trust that it is true. If you are finding it difficult to believe or trust; ask him for faith to believe; he will never turn you down.

Now that we are believing in Jesus' ability to save us and guide us (congratulations, by the way), let's grab some identity.

Everyone wants to think of identity statically, that is as if it has been established and cannot change. It would be more accurate if we were to describe identity dynamically. I mean by this that identity is in process, we are always becoming what we will be. Allowing this to be true, our identity is "becoming" more like Jesus.

> *You were taught, with regard to your former way of life, to put off your old self, which is being corrupted by its deceitful desires; [23]to be made new in the attitude of your minds; [24]and to put on the new self, created to be like God in true righteousness and holiness* **(Ephesians 4:22-24, TNIV).**

For the purposes of our investigation, the "former way of life" and the "old self" is bottom-up thinking. This way of life, this thinking, is being corrupted (spoiled, shriveled, withered, defiled, destroyed)[3], because it always begins with self, it is selfish! We may be somewhat altruistic (unselfish, devoted to another's best interest) but that is deceptive because we are always looking for a return on investment (ROI). We want to be thanked. We want to be recognized for being unselfish. We want someone to put us first, etc. This corrupting influence will never lead to true God-type love which is unselfish, sacrificial, and never looks for repayment. This (old self) identity is sensual, having only to do with what we can see, hear, smell, taste, and touch; what is here and now. This way of thinking, no matter how we state it revolves around us. The more we think about ourselves the deeper we descend into despair for there is nothing good, no moral goodness at the bottom. Therefore, Paul said to the Ephesians that this "former way of life," this "old self" is BEING corrupted by its deceitful desires. The desires of the bottom-up self are deceiving us into thinking good is bad, and bad is good. For example, think of situational ethics. These are a system of ethical principles guided by the immediate situation. In this understanding and practice of behavior the "right" and "wrong" are determined not by rule or law, but by the situation itself. Moral relativity is a sister to situational ethics. This is a system of morality that is relative to the immediate situation or circumstance. This is the essence of bottom-up thinking.

The next phrase *to be made new in the attitude of your minds* is quite refreshing. It is a great contrast from *being corrupted by its deceitful desires*. First, it is in the passive voice. English verbs have one of two "voices." Active voice means that the subject is doing something. Passive voice means that the action is being done to the subject. In this phrase, God is making your mind think in new ways. Read it again. You cannot begin to think top-down until your attitude, that is your mental stance or posture has changed. What is meant here is that you now think of God first, instead of self. Your thinking begins with God. What is he doing in this situation? How would he have me serve him in this instance? How can I join him in what he is doing? Some translations use the words "spirit of your minds" instead of "attitude of your minds." It makes little difference. The action of God is in the changing of your direction; away from self and toward God. Now we switch to active voice. We must do something. This is up to us, *to put on the new self, created to be like God in true righteousness and holiness*. We must put on this new self. This means that we must begin to think, now that our attitudes have been changed, from the top down. This new self is created to be like God! How? In true righteousness (right thinking and doing) and holiness (purity). A valid question at this point might be to ask; how is it that God is not selfish? He wants us to love him, he wants us to bring him glory, to honor and praise him. That seems self-centered to me. That is an excellently crafted question, well done. The answer would be that God is loveable, God is glorious, God is honorable, and he is praiseworthy; all on his own. We are not. Furthermore, God created. He did not need anything; therefore, creation was an act of other-centeredness. Once we chose to disobey him (sin, the fall of man), he did not need to save us. Read Philippians 2 for further study, it tells of Jesus leaving glory, becoming a man, dying a horrible death, etc. all to save us (more in chapter 3)! These are all very unselfish actions of a perfect, holy, complete, and righteous God. Not only this, but he gives us new thinking (top-down), gives us a new self (born-again) which is created and being re-created to be like God; righteous and holy. All of which we could in no way do on our own! Because of Jesus we can begin to think with our new identity as he dynamically changes our thinking from self to God, from bottom-up to top-down.

QUESTIONS TO PROVOKE CHANGE

1. What spiritual reality is required for top-down thinking? Which do you want to be?

2. Think about or discuss the importance of Jesus' incarnation (the joining of the realm of the 5 senses with the spiritual realm) regarding top-down thinking.

3. "Bottom-up thinking is particularly destructive and gives a false identity." Why is it destructive? Why is a true identity important? What is the remedy?

4. "The foremost identifier of you is you!" Why is this true from the bottom-up? Why is this true from the top-down?

5. God is pleased to have you in his family. What significance is that to you?

6. Describe bottom-up thinking and the results.

7. How does putting off your 'old self' and putting on the 'new self' relate to top-down thinking?

Notes and Thoughts:

CHAPTER 2
OUT OF THE HEART THE MOUTH SPEAKS

In the context of the passage of Scripture (Luke 6:27-45), Jesus is speaking to his disciples, at this time, there were many more than the twelve. He spoke of loving even their enemies, not judging other's behavior, doing good to those who hate you, etc. His words were in stark contrast of bottom-up thinking. Read the entire passage for full effect.

> *Good people bring good things out of the good stored up in their heart, and evil people bring evil things out of the evil stored up in their heart. <u>For out of the overflow of the heart the mouth speaks</u>* **(Luke 6:45,** TNIV**).**

This is the culmination of what Jesus was teaching in Luke 6. What is inside of you is what will come out, especially come out in your speech! In our understanding, the evil inside people brings forth evil; bottom-up thinking approaches evil. Top-down thinking is always good because it is from God's perspective. Let's investigate a biblical example of this kind of thinking and utterance.

> *The LORD appeared to Abraham near the great trees of Mamre while he was sitting at the entrance to his tent in the heat of the day. ²Abraham looked up and saw three men*

standing nearby. When he saw them, he hurried from the entrance of his tent to meet them and bowed low to the ground.
³He said, "If I have found favor in your eyes, my lord, do not pass your servant by. ⁴Let a little water be brought, and then you may all wash your feet and rest under this tree. ⁵Let me get you something to eat, so you can be refreshed and then go on your way—now that you have come to your servant." "Very well," they answered, "do as you say."
⁶So Abraham hurried into the tent to Sarah. "Quick," he said, "get three seahs of the finest flour and knead it and bake some bread."
⁷Then he ran to the herd and selected a choice, tender calf and gave it to a servant, who hurried to prepare it. ⁸He then brought some curds and milk and the calf that had been prepared, and set these before them. While they ate, he stood near them under a tree.
⁹"Where is your wife Sarah?" they asked him. "There, in the tent," he said.
¹⁰Then the LORD said, "I will surely return to you about this time next year, and Sarah your wife will have a son."
Now Sarah was listening at the entrance to the tent, which was behind him. ¹¹Abraham and Sarah were already very old, and Sarah was past the age of childbearing. ¹²So Sarah laughed to herself as she thought, "After I am worn out and my lord is old, will I now have this pleasure?"
¹³Then the LORD said to Abraham, "Why did Sarah laugh and say, 'Will I really have a child, now that I am old?' ¹⁴Is anything too hard for the LORD? I will return to you at the appointed time next year and Sarah will have a son."
¹⁵Sarah was afraid, so she lied and said, "I did not laugh." But he said, "Yes, you did laugh **(Genesis 18:1-15,** TNIV).

What takes place in this passage is called a "theophany." A

theophany is a substantial, visual appearance of the Lord, usually for the purpose of revealing something. In this case affirming God's earlier promise that Abraham would become the "father of nations." For a deeper understanding read **Genesis 17**. Here, God visits Abraham at ninety-nine years old, Sarah was eighty-nine. God tells him that a year hence he shall have a son by Sarah. There is no indication that Abraham doubted! Rather, he might have laughed with joy. God had made him believe and Abraham responded by thinking top-down and did everything God commanded. He circumcised every male under his control, **Genesis 17**. No small feat! The purpose of our using this passage is Sarah. Sarah overheard God's promise that she would bear a son, even in her old age. She doubted. She was thinking bottom-up. She was listening to the tapes in her head from her family, her culture, and herself that she was worthless because she was childless; that no matter what she did it was not good enough to give her the reward of a child. What was in her heart came out of her mouth, she laughed. It would seem that she laughed in hopeless, sarcastic derision, perhaps scorn. When she was caught, she lied, and she was rebuked by God. Remember, what God says: that he will do. A year later Isaac was born of Sarah.

> *Sarah said, "God has brought me laughter, and everyone who hears about this will laugh with me." ⁷And she added, "Who would have said to Abraham that Sarah would nurse children? Yet I have borne him a son in his old age* **(Genesis 21:6-7,** TNIV).

Out of the heart, the mouth speaks. Sarah is now speaking from what fills her heart; God, true and faithful. She is now thinking top-down! **And she has a new identity!**

Now we turn to a man in transition from bottom-up, hopeless, to top-down, faithful, thinking. A man brought his son, who could not speak because of an evil spirit. This spirit would frequently seize him and try to throw him into fire or water to drown him, foaming at the mouth, gnashing his teeth, and causing him to go rigid. Jesus had just come from the mount of transfiguration; his disciples who were ministering at the base of the mound, could not provide remedy. The father, who for many years, doubtlessly had great concern for his son brought him to Jesus.

> *So they brought the boy. But when the evil spirit saw Jesus, it threw the child into a violent convulsion, and he fell to the ground, writhing and foaming at the mouth. [21] "How long has this been happening?" Jesus asked the boy's father. He replied, "Since he was a little boy. [22] The spirit often throws him into the fire or into water, trying to kill him. Have mercy on us and help us, if you can." [23] "What do you mean, 'If I can'?" Jesus asked. "Anything is possible if a person believes." 24 The father instantly cried out, "I do believe, but help me overcome my unbelief!"* **(Mark 9:20-24,** NLT**).**

In the days of Jesus, it was commonly believed that if children had any kind of malady it was because of their parent's sin. As a good father, we know nothing of the mother, he would have tried every remedy known to man at the time, nothing helped. We assume he had heard of Jesus' healings and miracles, it appears he had heard that Jesus's disciples had been healing as well. His first request is astute, *"have mercy on us and help us,"* both of us, gives insight into how he is thinking. Then, he adds *"if you can."* Hope is not faith, yet this man is there, asking; indicating that he is not completely hopeless. Jesus challenges him and the man responds magnificently. *"I do believe, help me overcome my unbelief."* **If only we would pray that prayer more often!** How could God in the flesh, do anything but answer that prayer? Of course, the end of the account is that the boy is delivered and healed. That is great! But the main miracle is the prayer and God's answer to it. The man had made a transition from bottom-up to top-down thinking for a moment. It takes many of these transitional moments to finally become a top-down thinker. The father and son both had an identity adjustment. They now belonged to the family of the King of Kings and Lord of Lords.

> *The people were all so amazed that they asked each other, "What is this? A new teaching—and with authority! He even gives orders to evil spirits and they obey him"* **(Mark 1:27, TNIV)**.

In the account of the father and the afflicted boy, it was heavy duty adversity over some time that made the change. It usually takes some pain to get us to see clearly and to trust greatly.

> *And though the Lord give you the bread of adversity and the water of affliction, yet your Teacher will not hide himself anymore, but your eyes shall see your Teacher. ^{21} And your ears shall hear a word behind you, saying, "This is the way, walk in it," when you turn to the right or when you turn to the left. ^{22} Then you will defile your carved idols overlaid with silver and your gold-plated metal images. You will scatter them as unclean things. You will say to them, "Be gone!"* **(Isaiah 30:20-22, ESV)**.

Stubbornness: It is one of the marks of the fallen human nature. We do not learn quickly. God is patient with us, thankfully. Sometimes it seems he wants us to be like Jesus more than we do ourselves, yet he draws us to himself. My mentor and teacher, Ralph H. Weaver said to me one day when I was resisting what he was teaching me, probably frustrating him to craziness, "Boy, you can learn, or you can get taught." Wow! What a lesson in eight words! Learning is relatively painless but getting taught always involves some degree of pain. It is the same with top-down thinking. We are going to do it. We can learn to do it, or we can be taught to do it. What a gracious, loving, merciful God we serve. Isaiah was speaking to Israel in a rebellious time of their history. They had begun, again, to worship idols. That is, to depend on created objects rather than the creator of all objects. They also had philosophies, religions, institutions, etc. just as we do. Bottom-up thinking depends on these things, relies on them for peace and joy, hopes in them. But they cannot deliver; they never have and they never will. In the passage above, when adversity and affliction come; turn first to the Teacher, listen to him, he knows the way and stands ready to direct you. THIS IS TOP-DOWN THINKING! Then you can scatter the unclean things, bottom-up thinking, and say, 'Be gone.' This means that we can live in this world, understanding all its ways and means, sciences and philosophies; but not be governed by them or rely on them. When we see from God's perspective, we have HOPE, for how can God be hopeless?

> *See to it that no one takes you captive through hollow and deceptive philosophy, which depends on human tradition and the elemental spiritual forces of this world rather than on Christ* **(Colossians 2:8,** TNIV).

Paul warns us that we can begin to rely on what men think and teach *hollow and deceptive philosophy*. When they teach it long enough it becomes a tradition *human tradition* and we rely on it. Things like government, education, medicine, technology, philosophy, etc. are examples of such traditions. None of these are wrong or evil in themselves but when we rely on them to guide us, when we depend on them to protect us, and when we look for love, joy, peace, and happiness in these things; we are on the wrong road. See to it that no one, not even yourself, takes you captive to these things. If we consult the *elemental spiritual forces of this world* (cards, dice, Ouija, palmistry, horoscopes, etc.) even in "jest" we are thinking bottom-up and it will come to no good. Paul sums it all up *"rather than on Christ."* Be taken captive by him; God who knows all, God who is all-powerful, and God who is everywhere. Trust all outcomes of his to come to good. Begin to see with his eyes, think his thoughts, say his words, and do his deeds. THIS IS TOP-DOWN THINKING.

Out of the heart the mouth speaks.

> *If you declare with your mouth, "Jesus is Lord," and believe in your heart that God raised him from the dead, you will be saved. 10For it is with your heart that you believe and are justified, and it is with your mouth that you profess your faith and are saved* **(Romans 10:9-10,** TNIV).

With our hearts, we believe trusting that God is who he says he is in all the Bible, and are justified, thinking right and doing right, and our mouths speak it! I am saved first, from myself; then saved from this world; then saved from the enemy who would destroy me; but most of all saved to know God personally, to my capacity. My capacity to know God is a process, it is growing. More top-down thinking creates more trust in God himself. The same is true for all who will dare to think top-down.

QUESTIONS TO PROVOKE CHANGE

1. What can you learn about yourself by analyzing your speech?

2. What indicated Sarah's conversion from bottom-up thinking to top-down thinking?

3. Out of the demon-possessed boy's father came a prayer to Jesus. How does this prayer help you and how does it show top-down thinking?

4. "It usually takes some pain to get us to see clearly and to trust greatly." What does this sentence mean to you?

5. How does Colossians 2:8 impact you and your thinking?

Notes and Thoughts:

F. Michael Grubbs

CHAPTER 3
LANGUAGE IS THE DIAGNOSTIC INDICATOR

That is what the Scriptures mean when they say, "No eye has seen, no ear has heard, and no mind has imagined what God has prepared for those who love him." 10 But it was to us that God revealed these things by his Spirit. For his Spirit searches out everything and shows us God's deep secrets. 11 No one can know a person's thoughts except that person's own spirit, and no one can know God's thoughts except God's own Spirit. 12 And we have received God's Spirit (not the world's spirit), so we can know the wonderful things God has freely given us. 13 When we tell you these things, we do not use words that come from human wisdom. Instead, we speak words given to us by the Spirit, using the Spirit's words to explain spiritual truths **(1 Corinthians 2:9-13,** NLT**)**.

Language is how you think. You think in words that correlate to idea, thought, object, etc. Therefore, language is not only between individuals or groups of people but it is personal, inside yourself. Think of a quality that you possess that others have told you about, and that you believe to be true. If you are told this often enough by others, but mostly by yourself, this becomes an "identifier." For instance, you look in the mirror and you see a crooked nose, others have told you that you have a crooked nose; both others telling you about your nose and the mirror confirming it "identify" you as a person with a crooked nose. Now think; are you a person with a crooked nose, or are you a crooked-nosed person? What if you are told repeatedly that you are stupid, worthless, good-for-nothing, a failure, and you begin to believe this about yourself! If this plays in your head long enough your "identity" becomes; a stupid, worthless, good-for-nothing, failure person. Now think, are you a person, or are you those qualities? Some people have been told and come to believe that they are the greatest thing that has ever been. All their words should be recorded for posterity, their thoughts are better than any mortal's thoughts and they are to be taken seriously. They should always succeed. They, in fact, are the center of all things. If you know someone like this, you probably think they are deluded, but no more so than the first example. What others think of us, and what we think of ourselves and others, is actually of the least value. It is all bottom-up thinking and amounts to nothing. **What matters is what God thinks!** This can be trusted. This is valuable. What God thinks; creates your TRUE IDENTITY!

> *Because of the privilege and authority God has given me, I give each of you this warning: Don't think you are better than you really are. Be honest in your evaluation of yourselves, measuring yourselves by the faith God has given us* **(Romans 12:3,** TNLT**).**

In this verse Paul gives us an admonition (gentle correction). When most people read this verse, they suppose it to mean, 'do not get big-headed.' Let's look a little closer. *"Don't think you are better than you really are."* Straightforward, no big head, got it. The next sentence is more telling, *"Be honest in your evaluation of yourselves."* This means reality! Only God can see what is truly real, we get impressions of it, usually foggy, but he sees the real thing! And he tells us what it is.

> *For God knew his people in advance, and he chose them to become like his Son, so that his Son would be the firstborn*

among many brothers and sisters. ³⁰ And having chosen them, he called them to come to him. And having called them, he gave them right standing with himself. And having given them right standing, he gave them his glory **(Romans 8:29-30, NLT)**.

This is your identity as God sees you! When and only when you begin to see top-down will you be on the way to becoming what God already sees! God, omniscient (all-knowing) knew his people in advance. Remember:

Even before he made the world, God loved us and chose us in Christ <u>to be holy and without fault in his eyes</u> **(Ephesians 1:4, TNIV)**.

Another way of saying this might be: God sees, with his eyes, you, becoming holy and without fault! (To refresh yourself, see Chapter 1 of this book). This statement is mind-boggling. Take it exactly as it is, but substitute your name for "us." Let me summarize Romans 8:29-30: Known by God, chosen to be Christ-like, Jesus our perfect older brother. Chosen, called, justified, right standing, glorified (future). This is your IDENTITY.

- <u>Known and loved by God</u> –*Long ago the LORD said to Israel: "I have loved you, my people, with an everlasting love. With unfailing love I have drawn you to myself* **(Jeremiah 31:3, NLT)**.
- <u>Chosen to be Christ-like</u> –*And because of his glory and excellence, he has given us great and precious promises. These are the promises that enable you to share his divine nature and escape the world's corruption caused by human desires* **(2 Peter 1:4, NLT)**.
- <u>Called</u> –*But you are a chosen people, a royal priesthood, a holy nation, God's special possession, that you may declare the praises of him who called you out of darkness into his wonderful light* **(1 Peter 2:9, NLT)**.
- <u>Justified</u> (right standing) –*So now there is no condemnation for those who belong to Christ Jesus* **(Romans 8:1, NLT)**.

- <u>Glorified</u> (future) – (Jesus' prayer) *I have given them the glory that you gave me, that they may be one as we are one—* (**John 17:22**. NLT).

This is your IDENTITY! This is reality. Top-down thinking begins with God and looks at circumstance. Bottom-up thinking begins with circumstance and may or may not consider God into the equation.

LANGUAGE IS THE DIAGNOSTIC INDICATOR

Remember, words matter; out of the heart the mouth speaks. Listen to your language. Where do you begin? If it is with circumstance, the environment surrounding (circum) where you are standing (stance); you are thinking bottom-up. Sentences beginning with "I," will demonstrate this. I am sick. I should… I need… I ought, etc. Sentences beginning with "you" will demonstrate bottom-up thinking. You should… you need to… you ought to…. etc. The same is true for he/she sentences. Sentences beginning with things demonstrate bottom-up thinking. This crappy job… this lousy weather… this rotten relationship…. etc. You get the idea. Now it is impossible to begin every sentence with God, but a considerable number of your thoughts and spoken sentences should include him, should be from his perspective. As I write this, I have a double ear infection, a sore throat, a severe head cold (using lots of tissues), and pink eye! I wonder what God is teaching me through this trying time of my physical life? DID YOU SEE IT? The description began with "I" words, but the question is from TOP-DOWN!

When we finally begin to see ourselves as God sees us, our identity, and begin to speak as if Jesus is the center of all things and not us; then we will begin to THINK top-down. Top-down thinking includes God in every thought.

> *For the weapons of our warfare are not of the flesh but have divine power to destroy strongholds. ⁵ We destroy arguments and every lofty opinion raised against the knowledge of God, and take every thought captive to obey*

Christ,
(2 Corinthians 10:4-5, ESV).

When we speak, generally people listen. The listeners are either man-centered or God-centered. Contrary to modern Christian thinking Satan is not our biggest enemy, we are, ourselves! And the stronghold of the battle is our thinking. Bottom-up thinking is destructive and disastrous. But the weapons with which we fight are DIVINE (belonging to God) and able to destroy this bottom-up stronghold. See the beginning of verse **5**; *We destroy arguments and every lofty opinion raised against the knowledge of God,* all bottom-up thinking argues and opines against God being in control, being the center, being all-important. See the end of verse **5**; *and take every thought captive to obey Christ,* THIS IS TOP-DOWN THINKING. This places Jesus in control: what is he doing in this instance? This makes Jesus the center: how can I join him in what he is doing? This makes him all-important in every circumstance.

In your relationships with one another, have the same attitude of mind Christ Jesus had: **(Philippians 2:5, TNIV).**

The Greek word for attitude here is translated "mind" or "thinking" (as well as elsewhere in the New Testament and in other translations of this verse). In this passage verses **1-4** are about unity of thinking and acting in all Christ-followers. Verses 6 and following show Jesus' humility. We are to think like Jesus, who submitted himself, not to circumstance but to God. **Read the entire passage. It is important**. Paul is saying; think Christ's thoughts. Think the way Jesus thought. This is top-down thinking. **How you speak will be the diagnostic indicator of what is in your heart!** Listen to yourself and begin to change your language to top-down. Every time you correct yourself your heart gets changed into Jesus' heart. The mind (thinking) follows, then your speech will be pleasing to God and you will glorify him.

May the words of my mouth and the meditation of my heart

> *be pleasing to you, O LORD, my rock and my redeemer* **(Psalm 19:14,** NLT**)**.

This change is not like a light switch. It is on, then off. This change will take effort on your part. You must pay attention to your language, make many adjustments and corrections. Every time you do, your mind will be changed from bottom-up to top-down thinking. The Holy Spirit will convict you and guide you, if you ask him. The rewards are tremendous. Enlist others who have the same desire. Help each other by gentle correction. Always remember Paul's encouragement to Timothy:

> *A servant of the Lord must not quarrel but must be kind to everyone, be able to teach, and be patient with difficult people. ^{25} Gently instruct those who oppose the truth. Perhaps God will change those people's hearts, and they will learn the truth. ^{26} Then they will come to their senses and escape from the devil's trap. For they have been held captive by him to do whatever he wants* **(2 Timothy 2:24-26,** NLT**)**.

Now, let us take up this chapter's opening text:

> *However, as it is written: "What no eye has seen, what no ear has heard, and what no human mind has conceived— these things God has prepared for those who love him"— ^{10}for God has revealed them to us by his Spirit. The Spirit searches all things, even the deep things of God. ^{11}For who knows a person's thoughts except that person's own spirit within? In the same way no one knows the thoughts of God except the Spirit of God. ^{12}We have not received the spirit of the world but the Spirit who is from God, that we may understand what God has freely given us. ^{13}This is what we speak, not in words taught us by human wisdom but in words taught by the Spirit, explaining spiritual realities with Spirit-taught words* **(1 Corinthians 2:9-13,** TNIV**)**.

God has revealed to us, by his Spirit (top-down) what no human eye has seen, what no human ear has heard, and what no human mind has conceived or imagined. No amount of bottom-up thinking could arrive at this revelation! Not the highest human intelligence could conceive what God freely gives! The spirit of the world (bottom-up) could not reveal it. Only the Spirit who is from God (top-down) can help us understand what God freely gives us. **This means that only God can give us himself. He does this through his Spirit**. All that he is, all that he is doing can only be known by him revealing it (top-down). Which he does! [13]*This is what we speak, not in words taught us by human wisdom but in words taught by the Spirit, explaining spiritual realities with Spirit-taught words*. LANGUAGE IS THE DIAGNOSTIC INDICATOR to demonstrate whether you are still thinking bottom-up or are now thinking top-down. Begin this journey today. As you practice it, it will become more and more habit. Eventually someone will say, "nice weather we are having," and your immediate response will be something like "The Lord's mercies are new every morning." Your thinking is changing already!

QUESTIONS TO PROVOKE CHANGE

1. "What God thinks creates your true identity." How does this sentence impact you?

2. The words you speak in everyday life indicate your thinking; bottom-up or top-down, how will you monitor this?

3. Discuss your identity as God sees you (Romans 8:29-30).

4. How is language a "diagnostic" indicator of how you are thinking?

5. Contemplate the meaning of 1 Corinthians 2:9-13 in the light of top-down thinking?

Notes and Thoughts:

F. Michael Grubbs

PART Two
PURPOSE: CHANGE THE WORDS, CHANGE THE MIND

F. Michael Grubbs

CHAPTER 4
THE ATTITUDE OF JESUS

As we have seen in Part 1 of this book our identity is shaped by what we believe in our hearts about God, who he is and his attitude toward us. This demands a change in how we think which in turn changes our language regarding ourselves and others, both self-talk and outward speech. In Part 2 we shall investigate purpose. We will use the terms purpose and significance. Purpose, why we are here and what we are supposed to be doing. Significance, our importance and value. These words describe how we fit into the Kingdom of God and our mission in this world. There is generic purpose, that which every Christ-follower is called to be and do. There is specific purpose, that which is unique to you, how God made you, gifted you, and his plan for you. We will investigate both generic purpose and specific purpose in Part 2.

> *Is there any encouragement from belonging to Christ? Any comfort from his love? Any fellowship together in the Spirit? Are your hearts tender and compassionate? ² Then make me truly happy by agreeing wholeheartedly with each other, loving one another, and working together with one mind and purpose. ³Don't be selfish; don't try to impress others. Be humble, thinking of others as better than yourselves. ⁴ Don't look out only for your own interests, but take an interest in others, too. ⁵You must have the same*

attitude that Christ Jesus had. ⁶ *Though he was God, he did not think of equality with God as something to cling to.* ⁷ *Instead, he gave up his divine privileges; he took the humble position of a slave and was born as a human being. When he appeared in human form,* ⁸ *he humbled himself in obedience to God and died a criminal's death on a cross.* ⁹ *Therefore, God elevated him to the place of highest honor and gave him the name above all other names.* ¹⁰ *that at the name of Jesus every knee should bow, in heaven and on earth and under the earth,* ¹¹ *and every tongue declare that Jesus Christ is Lord, to the glory of God the Father* **(Philippians 2:1-11,** NLT**).**

This passage of Scripture has many books written about it. We do not have time or space to develop it here, nor is it the purview of this book. However, there are some significant points to consider. Paul writes to the church at Philippi; he outlines his hopes and expectations for how they should establish themselves in their city as Christ followers and top-down thinkers (verses **1-4**). In verses 1-2 he sets the stage for top-down thinking. Do you see it? It takes the form of an if…then statement. The NIV makes this point more clearly; *Therefore **if** you have any encouragement from being united with Christ, **if** any comfort from his love, **if** any common sharing in the Spirit, **if** any tenderness and compassion,* ²***then*** *make my joy complete by being like-minded, having the same love, being one in spirit and of one mind.* Our unification with Jesus should give us purpose; to be like-minded (top-down thinkers), loving, unified in spirit (born again) and of one mind (thinking top-down). Verses **3** and **4** instruct us in humility. Humility is not thinking of ourselves as unworthy, but understanding our place, putting others before, yielding to their interests, if everyone did this to everyone else, no one would be higher or lower than his brother or sister.

⁵***You must have the same attitude that Christ Jesus had****.*

Jesus' attitude (his stance, his posture) was submission to his

Father. *When he appeared in human form, [8] **he humbled himself in obedience to God** and died a criminal's death on a cross*. Bear with me here; before creation, before time, God in his three persons (the Trinity), Father, Word, and Spirit agreed that the Word would become flesh (JESUS).

> *So the Word became human and made his home among us. He was full of unfailing love and faithfulness. And we have seen his glory, the glory of the Father's one and only Son* **(John 1:14,** NLT**)**.

The Word became a man, Jesus, out of obedience to this decision! Because of his obedience, we are saved! Because of Jesus' top-down thinking we have an example that shows us how to think! Let me give you some more examples.

> *Jesus gave them this answer: "Very truly I tell you, the Son can do nothing by himself; he can do only what he sees his Father doing, because whatever the Father does the Son also does* **(John 5:19,** TNIV**)**.

Jesus was so in tune with the Father that the Father's thinking and doing were clear to him. And that is what he did.

> *I don't speak on my own authority. The Father who sent me has commanded me what to say and how to say it. 50 And I know his commands lead to eternal life; so I say whatever the Father tells me to say"* **(John 12:49,** TNIV**)**.

Jesus, as a man (God also, but in the flesh) was so united with the Father that he only spoke what he heard the Father say! **Out of the heart the mouth speaks**. Finally, the result; God elevated him above every name! The highest honor! And every knee will bow and every tongue confess that he is LORD. Some to glory, some to their disgrace. Well, what is our reward if we recognize his changing of our hearts, our top-down thinking, and the language that reflects our union with Jesus?

> *And the God of all grace, who called you to his eternal*

glory in Christ, after you have suffered a little while, will himself restore you and make you strong, firm and steadfast. ¹¹To him be the power for ever and ever. Amen **(1 Peter 5:10-11, TNIV)**.

Read this verse slowly and carefully.

- God of all grace (without his un-earned favor we have nothing)
- Called to his (God's own) eternal glory in Jesus (every knee will bow…)
- After suffering briefly (struggling to think top-down)
- God himself! Will restore you strong, firm, and steadfast.

This is PURPOSE; generic, for all Christ-Followers: That, in Union with Jesus we will be strong, standing firm, remaining steadfast as a testimony to our Great God and Savior, Jesus Christ!

QUESTIONS TO PROVOKE CHANGE

1. Discuss the difference between "generic" purpose and "specific" purpose. Why is this important to you?

2. How did Jesus himself demonstrate top-down thinking? How does his demonstration inspire or motivate you?

Notes and Thoughts:

CHAPTER 5
GOD'S WILL FOR YOU (GENERIC)

As a pastor for many years and a pastoral counselor for more years, there is one almost universal question every believer asks. **What is God's will for my life?** A very good question! This question must be answered in two ways. First, what is God's will for me? Second, what does God want to do with me? In this chapter, we will answer the first question.

God's will for you is written many times in Scripture. The most succinct is found in:

> *God's will is for you to be holy,*
> **(1 Thessalonians 4:3a,** NLT**).**

Holy has two meanings 1) pure, 2) other; God is pure (he is light and in him is no darkness), he is other (there is nothing like him, nothing even to compare to him). God is making us pure, and other than what we were: holy! The definition of sovereignty, simply understood is: "God gets it his way," whatever he wants! For some, this is difficult because it seems that, if God is good, he is not getting it his way. Though understandable, this thinking is bottom-up. We are finite. We can only see a few feet in front of us. We do not see the whole picture. And being arrogant and rebellious, we think we know better than God. Listen to the prophet Isaiah:

> *Do not forget this! Keep it in mind! Remember this, you guilty ones. ⁹ Remember the things I have done in the past. For I alone am God! I am God, and there is none like me. ¹⁰ Only I can tell you the future before it even happens. Everything I plan will come to pass, for I do whatever I wish* **(Isaiah 46:8-10,** NLT**)**.

If you desire to learn more about God's sovereignty (and I hope you will), read **Job 38:1-42:6**. Here, Job is converted from bottom-up thinking to top-down thinking. Job got taught! It is God's will that you be made holy; therefore, holy you will be! That is his generic purpose for you. That is what he is doing in your life. What he begins he will finish.

> *And I am certain that God, who began the good work within you, will continue his work until it is finally finished on the day when Christ Jesus returns* **(Philippians 1:6,** NLT**)**.

This is very good news! It tells us that God is not waiting to pounce on you for every sinful thought, every sinful word, every sinful deed. He has already dealt with your sin, on the cross. **He is making you holy!** His Spirit convicts you of sin; you must confess (acknowledge) your sin and repent (turn away from sin and toward God), and in this way, we respond to his purpose for us: to become holy!

> *But now you must be holy in everything you do, just as God who chose you is holy. ¹⁶ For the Scriptures say, "You must be holy because I am holy"* **(1 Peter 1:15-16,** NLT**)**.

A Renewed Mind

> *And so, dear brothers and sisters, I plead with you to give your bodies to God because of all he has done for you. Let them be a living and holy sacrifice—the kind he will find acceptable. This is truly the way to worship him. ²Don't*

copy the behavior and customs of this world, <u>but let God transform you into a new person by changing the way you think</u>. Then you will learn to know God's will for you, which is good and pleasing and perfect **(Romans 12:1-2, NLT)**.

These two verses are crucial to top-down thinking regarding God's purpose in your life. Paul is writing to the Roman church and urging them *to give your bodies to God*. Here "bodies" means more than arms and legs. It literally means your whole being, your whole self. Because of all he has done for you, in view of his love, sacrifice, mercy, grace, adoption and much more; give your whole self to God as a living and holy sacrifice, an offering. Only when you have given it all to him will it be acceptable. Do not worry if you think this impossible, remember, **God is making you holy**; therefore, he will remind you of what you have withheld until you finally yield it all to him. God will have all of you or none of you. He chooses to have all of you. As we make this sacrifice of our total being, more and yet more, to the only great and glorious God: **we worship him!** This worship is an ongoing action for all eternity. Let it begin now!

When you offer him more and more of you, you cease to think from the bottom up! *Don't copy the behavior and customs of this world* is the next phrase in our passage. Today's New International Version (TNIV) translates it: *Do not conform to the pattern of this world*, taking the two translations together makes the understanding a little deeper. What it is really saying is STOP THINKING BOTTOM-UP! The pattern of this world is thinking that our knowledge (science), our systems of thought (philosophy), and our social systems (legal, medical, educational, religious, political, etc.) can solve the world's problems, given enough time and effort. Copying these behaviors and customs will NEVER solve our problems. We have been trying to do it since Adam and Eve! It has not worked yet! Does this mean that we should not have tried? No! It means that what we have learned, how we have organized societies is of great value, **but it is not of the most importance**. Let me give a simple example. You were in a hurry and were driving 55 in a 35 mile per hour zone. The lights in the rear-view mirror and the siren are telling you to pull over. You pull over. The officer gives you a speeding ticket summoning you to court. When you get home, you go on your computer and find a lawyer, who for $350 will get your ticket reduced to a malfunctioning tail light. The legal system has provided you a way to pay a fine (and a lawyer fee) to avoid the punishment of the law. However, perhaps you have not learned the lesson that God was trying to teach you. Therefore, you will have to learn it again! Certainly, a better way would have been to go home after you received the ticket approaching the LORD and inquiring of him what he is teaching you about your life, why you were late, why you thought you could break the law, etc.? The lawyer is only a temporary fix, and expensive. If you were directed by the Spirit and walking with him, perhaps you would not have been late, perhaps you could have made a phone call informing your office or appointment you would be late, etc. Thinking bottom-up is only dealing with the unpleasantness of sin; not dealing with sin itself. Top-down thinking (from God's perspective) deals with the core issue. Which is more important to you? According to the pattern of this world, all we think of is expediency and avoiding consequences. The renewed mind is going deeper; it is learning the life lessons God teaches. I regret the inadequacies of this example, but it will have to suffice. The same bottom-up thinking goes for all areas of our lives. Earlier I shared my situation with medical problems. Is it wrong to see a physician to help me get well? Absolutely not! But when I **first** think about it from God's perspective; what are you showing me here, what am I to learn about overextending myself to exhaustion, how can I better live my life so that my immune system is not weakened because of lack of rest and eating incorrectly? Once I have seen what God is about, then I am free to seek medical help. Taking antibiotics will help me get over the symptoms, but if I do not want to repeat this experience (and I do not) I must think top-down first. *Don't copy the behavior and customs of this world, but let God transform you into a new person by changing the way you think.*

    The word transform (meta-morpho-o) is the Greek word from which we get the English word metamorphosis. It means to change from one thing to another. In this case from a worldly thinker to a spiritual thinker; in our language from a bottom-up thinker to a top-down thinker. We become a new person, governed not by the world, but by God! **Changed by the way we think**. The result of giving our entire selves to God as an acceptable offering; which is worship, and being transformed into a new person by the way we now think, top-down, provides us with an understanding of God's will. The word "then" is important. First, you must give your entire self to God. Second, you must be transformed from bottom-up to top-down in your thinking.

> ***Then* *you will learn to know God's will for you*,** *which is good and pleasing and perfect.*

This provides purpose for our lives! We can now understand that we are not floating around in the world useless, hopeless, trying to figure it all out; but that there is a plan, there is a reason, there is a purpose for our lives that matters. In other words, significance! Importance! We are important to God; in fact, his will for us is good, pleasing, and perfect! Paul writes to Timothy about this:

> *In a large house there are articles not only of gold and silver, but also of wood and clay; some are for noble purposes and some for disposal of refuse. ^{21}Those who cleanse themselves from the latter will be instruments for noble purposes, made holy, useful to the Master and prepared to do any good work* **(2 Timothy 2:20-21, TNIV)**.

We who will begin, and continue, to think top-down will be instruments for noble purposes – made holy – useful to the Master! To be an instrument in the hands of Jesus, to serve him, prepared to do any good work: this is high purpose. This is what is planned for you. Begin thinking top-down.

QUESTIONS TO PROVOKE CHANGE

1. Discuss the two definitions for "holy." What is the importance of each definition to you?

2. God is making you holy. Discuss the aspects of this truth. Discuss how this impacts your thinking.

3. Romans 12:1-2 is key to understanding top-down thinking. Discuss the meaning of each word and phrase in regard to top-down thinking. The word "then" is ultra-important in this two-verse passage; why?

4. Top-down thinking changes us from vessels for refuse to noble use. Explain 2 Timothy 2:20-21 and why it is important.

Notes and Thoughts:

CHAPTER 6
GOD'S WILL FOR YOU (SPECIFIC)

In this chapter, we will answer the second question; what does God want to do with me? The question 'what does God want to do with me?' could be understood in different ways. It could mean God is going to put me somewhere. It could mean God is going to use me to do something. It could mean that God is doing something and wants me to participate with him in the doing. All these are good, taken from the top-down, and all these interpretations are valid for your study in this chapter. God is going to put you in close relationship with him! God has planned specific work for you to do! God is doing something and wants you to do it with him!

Paul quotes the prophet Isaiah writing:

> *However, as it is written: "What no eye has seen, what no ear has heard, and what no human mind has conceived—these things God has prepared for those who love him"* **(1 Corinthians 2:9,** TNIV).

Paul is saying that even in our wildest imaginings we cannot guess what God has prepared for us who love Jesus! This is a tall order. We can imagine a lot of good things even from the bottom up. Several important verses follow **(10-15)** but Paul concludes this passage in verse **16** for, *"Who has known the mind of the Lord so* *as to instruct him?"* ***But we have the mind of Christ.*** (TNIV) Here, Paul is saying that we are in no position to tell the Lord, anything. But he has given us the MIND OF CHRIST! **We can think TOP-DOWN!** It is possible to see, to hear, to understand what God has prepared for us who love him (read verse **9** again). Because he has given us the ability to think like Jesus we can think top-down. What do you mean by this, Mike? Simply that Jesus' Spirit dwells in you (**Romans 8:9**) and God is conforming you into Jesus' likeness (**Romans 8:29**). He has transformed you by the renewing of your mind (**Romans 12:2**), and you can now think top-down. [Notice: God is doing all of this, all we need do is cooperate!]

In Jesus' last conversations with his disciples before he went to the garden, Jesus tells us something very important.

> *I no longer call you servants, because servants do not know their master's business. Instead, I have called you friends, for everything that I learned from my Father I have made known to you* (**John 15:15,** TNIV).

The implication is that friends are let in on the Master's business. Jesus has shared everything with the disciples that the Father wanted him to make known to them. At the end of the prayer in Gethsemane, according to John's gospel, Jesus concludes his prayer:

> *Father, I want those you have given me to be with me where I am, and to see my glory, the glory you have given me because you loved me before the creation of the world. 25"Righteous Father, though the world does not know you, I know you, and they know that you have sent me. 26I have made you known to them, and will continue to make you known in order that the love you have for me may be in them and that I myself may be in them"* (**John 17:24-26,** TNIV).

'Be with me where I am' seated at the right hand of God's

majesty (the chair! More about this follows). Seeing his glory, his glory as the WORD of God, before creation! Knowing God himself! Jesus in us! This can only be understood by top-down thinking. We have been given mind of Christ! Paul, in his letter to the church at Ephesus:

> *In him we have redemption through his blood, the forgiveness of sins, in accordance with the riches of God's grace 8that he lavished on us. With all wisdom and understanding, 9he made known to us the mystery of his will according to his good pleasure, which he purposed in Christ,* **(Ephesians 1:7-9,** TNIV).

We are redeemed by Jesus' blood, forgiven, lavished in grace. He has made known to us the mystery of his will and it pleases him according to his good pleasure! His purpose in Christ Jesus is known to us! You could not even imagine these things thinking bottom-up. If you have understood this chapter so far, you are already beginning to think top-down.

God's Specific Will for YOU!

Now we turn our attention to God's specific will for you. I have no idea what God's specific will is for you, his purpose, what he wants to do with you. This is a good thing. I have a friend who is always telling me, "God loves you, but I have a plan for your life." Yikes! Of course, he is using a play on words as a joke, but too often bottom-up thinking actually believes this! I know God loves me (bottom-up thinking really wants to plan my life), but what I really want is God's plan for my life. And you do too! How do we find it?

This will require an exploration of several Scriptures. First, let me explain proof-texting. Proof-texting simply put, is getting an idea and finding biblical verses to support the idea. In my opinion, if this is not sinful it certainly is dangerous. I am going to share with you THE CHAIR. Since I do not have time or space in this book to provide exposition of each verse in its context, I will leave that to you. I am not proof-texting; but you need to make sure of this by reading the contexts of the verses for yourself.

THE CHAIR

> *My people have committed two sins: They have forsaken me, the spring of living water, and have dug their own cisterns, broken cisterns that cannot hold water* **(Jeremiah 2:13,** TNIV).

God, through the prophet, is declaring his people (we are his people) guilty regarding two sins. First, forsaking himself. God describes himself as the spring of living water. This living water is a metaphor used many times in Scripture. The thing to note is; the water is alive! and we have turned away from it. For our purposes, this living water could represent top-down thinking. His people have forsaken it. The second sin; they have dug their own cisterns (containers), broken cisterns that cannot maintain or hold water. For our purposes, this could be bottom-up thinking. Remember, bottom-up thinking only considers what can be experienced by the five senses. It includes all knowledge we can discern except the spiritual dimension where God is found. Picture it this way, the spring of living water is like an artesian well. An artesian well is water forced up many hundreds of feet by pressure. It is cool, clean, clear, pure, and vital. It is what bottled water ought to be. We turn away from this! The broken cistern could be understood as a concrete bird-bath in the back yard in August. The birds use it, they are not house-broken. In the bottom of it grows this green slimy substance. This is what we drink! Bottom-up thinking is like that, never satisfying, always sickening, never bringing peace. Remember the SPRING OF LIVING WATER. It will come in at the end of the chair teaching.

> *And God raised us up with Christ and seated us with him in the heavenly realms in Christ Jesus,* **(Ephesians 2:6,** TNIV**)**

When Jesus was resurrected, we were too! It is the event that enables us to be raised from the dead. I would love to talk about this at length, but if you will read **Ephesians 2:1-5** you will find that Paul is declaring us to be dead, spiritually dead. Our spirit is the part of man that died in the garden of Eden at man's fall. We are so dead spiritually that we can only think bottom-up. Then in verse 2:4 **God raises us up, makes us alive,** by his great grace! So, we are raised with Christ. **God then seats us with him**. Now, in my simplicity, I understand that to be seated one must have something to sit on. I consider this to be a chair. Where is my chair? My chair is with God **in the heavenly realms!** Now God, we are told by many Scriptures, sits on a throne in heaven, therefore I assume my chair to be before his throne with Jesus seated at his right hand. I picture this to be like a Hollywood director's chair, with my name across the back. The last phrase '**in Christ Jesus,**' is important. If I went to sit in my chair before the Holy God in my present state having both a new, resurrected, reborn nature, and a sinful nature; the blazing holiness of God would consume me. Paul includes 'in Christ Jesus,' because when I go to my chair before the Holy God I go enveloped, clothed, wrapped, sealed in Jesus' righteousness. Therefore, I am accepted and safe and secure.

If I were to invite you to meet me for a cup of coffee (or your favorite beverage) at a coffee shop at 9 am on Tuesday morning; it would be implied that we would drink our beverages and have conversation. Two people do not usually stare at each other while drinking coffee without conversing. It is the same with the chair. There will be conversation. This conversation will be completely top-down. You begin to see things from God's perspective when in the chair!

> *Let us then approach God's throne of grace with confidence, so that we may receive mercy and find grace to help us in our time of need* **(Hebrews 4:16,** TNIV**)**.

We are invited to the chair. 'Let us then approach God's throne of grace' is an invitation to come to the chair. 'With confidence' is how we are to be dressed to meet God. Another translation says 'boldly.'

> *So let us come boldly to the throne of our gracious God. There we will receive his mercy, and we will find grace to help us when we need it most* **(Hebrews 4:16,** NLT**)**.

Jesus has paid the price for us, with his blood, to come to the Father **without fear, guilt, or shame**. What do we receive when we go to the chair before God's throne? Mercy and grace to help us in our time of need, when we need it most. Wow! The question arises; when am I not in need? NEVER! But in the chair, I shall receive mercy and grace for my needs (top-down). **Specific purpose is one of my needs**. I will discover it in the chair and so will you!

> *Guard your steps when you go to the house of God. Go near to listen rather than to offer the sacrifice of fools, who do not know that they do wrong. ²Do not be quick with your mouth, do not be hasty in your heart to utter anything before God. God is in heaven and you are on earth, so let your words be few* **(Ecclesiastes 5:1-2,** TNIV**)**.

Most of my Christian life I have been taught to pray with my mouth (or silently with words in my head). The wisest man who ever lived (beside Jesus) Solomon says, be careful when you go to your chair. Go to listen! (this implies God is talking!) Don't talk too much. If we spend some time praying by talking only, and then say Amen, get up and go about our business; we have only half prayed. **THE LISTENING PART IS MUCH MORE IMPORTANT**. God wants to speak with you. He has much to share with you.

> *My sheep listen to my voice; I know them, and they follow me.* **(John 10:27,** NLT**)**

This amazing verse of Scripture tells us that Jesus is speaking to us (his sheep); we need to listen and obey, follow. It also tells us that he knows all about us, especially what we are becoming!

Top-down thinking will be authenticated by listening to God's utterance and confirmed by what he says in his written word. There are two Greek words that are translated into English as "word." **Logos** is the written word. **Rhema** is the uttered or spoken word. God speaks both. One will never contradict the other. They are both the "word" of God. We understand or should understand and know the Logos. We need to be better at listening for the Rhema. The chair is a place where we can hear the Rhema.

> *Then the angel showed me the river of the water of life, as clear as crystal, flowing from the throne of God and of the Lamb* **(Revelation 22:1,** TNIV).

Remember in Jeremiah when we turned away from the **spring** of living water? Now because of Jesus' love, mercy, and grace we are raised to new life and seated in a chair before the throne of God and of the Lamb. Out from under the throne issues a **RIVER** OF THE WATER OF LIFE that runs right past our chair! We turned away from the spring of living water, God runs a whole river of life past us. This is Grace! Do you think you might get a drink of living water? Do you think you might dive in? Do you think you might take a bucket of it back to this world and dump it on someone? **Oh, yes you can!**

Now a challenge! You will need a sheet of paper and a pencil or pen. I will endeavor to guide you into a drawing. This drawing is a picture of **Revelation Chapters 4 & 5**. It might be good to read those two chapters before we begin. Do not be afraid of the Book of Revelation. You are going to really like this.

Good. You are back. Now, in the center of the page make a small rectangle. Now divide the rectangle in half and make a Capital F on the left side; and a Capital J on the right side. **F** for Father and **J** for Jesus. This rectangle represents the throne. **The rest of the drawing will consist of concentric circles around the throne, each one outside the next**. Now, a half inch from the northwest corner make an X, do the same for each of the corners. These represent the Cherubim, God's fiercest creatures. One has the face of a man, one the face of an ox, one the face of a lion, and one the face of an eagle. They each have six wings and the wings are covered with eyes. The next circle out from the Cherubim, make 24 hash marks. These represent the 24 elders on 24 thrones.

We do not know who they are, but they are reverent. The next circle should be made by dots. Make the circle about an inch thick and fill it full of dots. These represent the myriad of angels (myriad means uncountable). These are not Hallmark's little chubby guys with bows and arrows. No! These are warriors with light swords. This is God's army with which he will destroy everything before he creates the New Heaven and the New Earth. The last circle should be many hundreds of little hash marks. These represent the host of heaven. These are all those who have gone ahead of us into heaven and await the return of Jesus. **FIND AND POINT TO WHERE YOUR CHAIR IS LOCATED**. Make a little chair drawing and put your name on it. Look at the drawing, (look at the snapshot of heaven that God gave to John in Revelation 4 & 5). **HOW IMPORTANT ARE YOU?** Invited to sit amid all this glory, before the Living God! Invited to hear him speak with you; now! Take some time, right now, to meditate on this experience.

The chair is a practice. You must **learn** to sit and listen. This is contrary to our culture. [There is an excellent book entitled *Chairtime* by Dan Southerland to help you get started. Check it out at Amazon Kindle Books.] When you begin to sit in your chair (a literal one here, and the spiritual one before God), two things will assault you. First, your thoughts, you will have every kind of thought come into your mind. Second, emotions, many hurts, sufferings, injuries, and offenses will flood your mind. An effective way to deal with these is to imagine a stack of frisbees beside your chair. You are sitting and "I've got to get the oil changed" comes into your mind. Grab a frisbee put the oil change thought on it and fling it. Repeat this with all thoughts and emotions until you are still before God. Now you are ready to listen.

God rarely speaks to me with an audible voice. More likely he will put a thought in my mind, one that I know I would never think; or he might bring me to a Scripture verse; or he might impress something in my soul; or remind me of a lyric from a song. **In every case I will KNOW that it did not come from me**. It is one thing to read Scripture or hear a sermon about how God loves you. IT IS QUITE ANOTHER THING TO HEAR HIM SAY IT TO YOU!

A brief word from my daughter, Charissa Burns, a practitioner of the chair. This regards her teaching my grandson about the chair and three sentences about her experience.

> The Chair and a 9-year-old:
> When my husband and I were in a small group and given the task to teach our 9-year-old son what it means to pray and listen. My dad's (Mike) teaching on the chair came to mind. So, I sat my son down. I told him to close his eyes and picture a chair. I asked what the chair looked like. He said, "a rocking chair with all the colors on it!" Next, I told him to picture another chair across from his chair. Then, I said, "Picture yourself sitting in your chair and when you look up Jesus is in the other chair in front of you." I kept quiet after this for a while, which was not easy. I sat there watching my child with his eyes closed and then it happened! He started rocking as if he were really in THE CHAIR! I asked him what he heard. This was when my heart skipped many beats. He responded, "It's so warm and comfy! Jesus really loves me." I urge you to visualize your chair and hear the words of Christ for yourself.
>
> My Chair:
> For me my chair and Jesus' chair are in a spotlight and I can't really see everything around me. I know that around me are the cherubim, the elders, the myriad of angels, and the saints who have gone before me; however, I can't see them. The focus, the spotlight, is on Jesus sitting with me.

It is in the chair that you will discover God's specific purpose for your life.

> *For we are God's handiwork, created in Christ Jesus to do good works, which God prepared in advance for us to do* **(Ephesians 2:10,** TNIV).

Let's break this verse down. We are God's handiwork. This Greek word literally means, that which is made; workmanship. We are made by God! Then we are created in Christ Jesus, this is a reference to our being "made alive," born again! For what purpose? To do good works! What good works? The very ones the Father God prepared in advance for us to do! Only God knows this purpose, his specific, special purpose for you. And only he can give it to you. And you can ONLY get it by LISTENING to him!

Part 1 of this book shows us our identity, it can only be understood by top-down thinking. Part 2 of this book has shown our generic purpose and how to find our specific purpose. This can only be discovered by top-down thinking. Let us see how top-down thinking directs our behavior in the 3rd part of this book.

QUESTIONS TO PROVOKE CHANGE

1. What does it mean to have the "mind of Christ?" How important is this to top-down thinking?

2. "Friends" are let in on the Master's business. Jesus told the disciples (and by his Spirit we are disciples also) all that the Father wanted them to know. How does this impact your thinking?

3. God has made known the mystery of his will to us. How? And how does he continue to do it?

4. Summarize the "Chair" teaching. Discuss the value of being intimately connected to God; being able to listen to his "voice."

5. After viewing your invited place, in your chair, in the midst of all that is described in Revelation 4 and 5; discuss your emotions.

6. Begin to practice the Chair. Let God supply your "specific will," your calling. Discuss this process with others.

Notes and Thoughts:

PART THREE
BEHAVIOR: LIVING TOP-DOWN IN A BOTTOM-UP WORLD

CHAPTER 7
FREED FROM SHACKLES

In Part 1 of this book we concluded that our identity is found and maintained by seeing ourselves through God's eyes (top-down) and not through our own eyes, other's eyes, or our culture's eyes (bottom-up). In Part 2 of this book we concluded that it is not possible for us to find God's purpose for us, the reason of our existence, by any other means than being transformed by the renewing of our minds (top-down thinking). In Part 3 we shall investigate how we should then live, that is, behave with our identity and purpose derived from thinking top-down. In this chapter, we will look at the freedom God intends for us and how that liberty changes our behavior. God makes us free FROM things such as sin, etc. but he also makes us free to believe, free to trust him in all things.

The Shackles of Bottom-Up Thinking

So I tell you this, and insist on it in the Lord, that you must no longer live as the Gentiles do, in the futility of their thinking. [18]They are darkened in their understanding and separated from the life of God because of the ignorance that is in them due to the hardening of their hearts. [19]Having lost all sensitivity, they have given themselves over to sensuality so as to indulge in every kind of impurity, and they are full of greed **(Ephesians 4:17-19,** TNIV**).**

In chapter 1 of this book we looked at this passage with an emphasis on identity and top-down thinking; here we emphasize behavior. The word "gentiles," defines individuals who are not Christ-followers. These people may be good people or not so good people as the world defines goodness. They may have a sense of worldly morality, meaning they are not earthly law-breakers. They may exercise common sense. They may be caring for those less fortunate, etc. To read these verses and assume that these are out-of-control hedonists (pleasure-seekers) is a mistake, though they may be. Christ-followers are not to live (behave) like them because their bottom-up thinking is futile. Webster defines futile: Serving no useful purpose, ineffective. Paul is writing to the church in Ephesus about God's purpose and is clearly saying that gentiles are only able to think bottom-up. There is a progression outlined here; futile thinking, darkened understanding, separated from God's life, ignorant, and finally hard-hearted. This progression is causative. Meaning the cause of this futility is a hardened heart toward God, a refusal to consider him as important, central, imperative. They discount God in their thinking, except perhaps to give lip-service to the idea of him. The hardened heart produces ignorance. Gentiles have no understanding of the realm of the spiritual and do not consider it to have importance, except in some new age sort of vague capacity, which is not spiritual at all. This ignorance, caused by the hard heart makes it impossible for them to know God.

> *The person without the Spirit does not accept the things that come from the Spirit of God but considers them foolishness, and cannot understand them because they are discerned only through the Spirit* **(1 Corinthians 2:14,** TNIV**).**

This futility (bottom-up thinking) is the only way they can think. The ignorant bottom-up thinker is disconnected from God's life, separated.

> *Jesus replied, "Very truly I tell you, no one can see the*

kingdom of God without being born again **(John 3:3,** NIV).

The word "see," in this verse, means perceive. The hardhearted, ignorant, separated person is unaware of the spiritual realm, of God himself and his governance of this world. This darkened (without light) understanding of things results in futility. Christ-followers are not to live this way! Verse **19** *Having lost all sensitivity, they have given themselves over to sensuality so as to indulge in every kind of impurity, and they are full of greed.* This verse regards sensitivity and the result. Having lost all sensitivity means they have no sense of the realm of the Spirit. No sense of God himself. No regard or fear of offending him. Therefore, they have given themselves over to sensuality. This means they behave according to the five senses; seeing, hearing, touching, smelling, and tasting. That is all they can know so that is all they pursue. The last phrase; *and they are full of greed*, refers not only to greed in the sense of money or possession, but more of selfishness. All bottom-up thinking begins with the self. Top-down thinking begins with God!

Freed from the Shackles to Think God's Thoughts

But that isn't what you learned about Christ. ^{21} Since you have heard about Jesus and have learned the truth that comes from him, ^{22} throw off your old sinful nature and your former way of life, which is corrupted by lust and deception. ^{23} Instead, let the Spirit renew your thoughts and attitudes. ^{24} Put on your new nature, created to be like God—truly righteous and holy. **(Ephesians 4:20-24,** NLT).

We are taught to stop thinking bottom-up, to put off that way of life which is being corrupted by selfish desires (lust and deception), that are full of empty promises of fulfillment. Rather, **we are free to think top-down**, ^{23} *Instead, let the Spirit renew your thoughts and attitudes*, putting on the NEW SELF! This new self is created to be like God: righteous and holy! <u>Our behavior, the way we live. must reflect this way of thinking.</u>

> *It is for freedom that Christ has set us free. Stand firm, then, and do not let yourselves be burdened again by a yoke of slavery* **(Galatians 5:1, TNIV)**.

In our context, you must understand that Jesus has set you free to think top down, from his perspective. This freedom demands that we stand firm in our renewed mind, thinking top-down. This freedom demands vigilance; **that we do not allow ourselves to be enslaved again by bottom-up thinking, only including God as an after-thought**. In the most difficult of times we MUST begin our thinking with God. That he is good. That he knows. That he loves. That he has a plan. That he is working all things for his good purposes. This is top-down thinking.

> *Furthermore, because we are united with Christ, we have received an inheritance from God, for he chose us in advance, and he makes everything work out according to his plan* **(Ephesians 1:11, NLT)**.

In Jesus, you were chosen! It was decided, according to God's will, that you should be his and he is working out everything in conformity with his purposes, according to his plan. How good is this? That we are free to think this way?

> *Jesus said to the people who believed in him, "You are truly my disciples if you remain faithful to my teachings. ^{32} And you will know the truth, and the truth will set you free." ^{33} "But we are descendants of Abraham," they said. "We have never been slaves to anyone. What do you mean, 'You will be set free'?" ^{34} Jesus replied, "I tell you the truth, everyone who sins is a slave of sin. ^{35} A slave is not a permanent member of the family, but a son is part of the family forever. ^{36} So if the Son sets you free, you are truly free*
> **(John 8:31-36, NLT)**.

This passage is indicative of what I am trying to demonstrate.

Jesus is speaking to those people *who had believed in him*. He challenges them to be faithful to his teaching (think top-down). He declares that if they do, they will know truth! And this truth will set them free. Top-down thinking sets us free from worldly thinking. Look at their response carefully. It is a bottom-up response. *"But we are descendants of Abraham," they said. "We have never been slaves to anyone. What do you mean, 'You will be set free'?"* Think now, at that very moment in history they are enslaved by Roman rule! Previously, they had been enslaved by the Egyptians, Babylonians, the Assyrians, and the Medes-Persians. But worse than this; they missed the whole point because they were thinking bottom-up. Jesus was speaking about their souls, not their bodies, their culture or their nation. So, he continues, he tells them plainly that he is speaking of sin's enslavement. He explains what they already know, that slaves are not part of the family heritage, but sons are part of the family. He is the chief Son and if he sets us free (to think top-down) we are indeed free. In the following verses **37-45**, you will see how he condemns bottom-up thinking, where it comes from, and their insistence on thinking this way. Remember these are Jews who had believed him! **Yes, it is entirely possible to be a believer in Jesus yet be trapped in bottom-up thinking**. Let me repeat:

> *It is for freedom that Christ has set us free. Stand firm, then, and do not let yourselves be burdened again by a yoke of slavery* **(Galatians 5:1,** TNIV).

We will look at one more passage of Scripture that demonstrates our freedom in top-down thinking versus bondage in bottom-up thinking.

> *Those who live according to the sinful nature have their minds set on what that nature desires; but those who live in accordance with the Spirit have their minds set on what the Spirit desires. ⁶The mind controlled by the sinful nature is death, but the mind controlled by the Spirit is life and peace. ⁷The sinful mind is hostile to God; it does not submit*

to God's law, nor can it do so. ⁸Those controlled by the sinful nature cannot please God. ⁹You, however, are not controlled by the sinful nature but are in the Spirit, if indeed the Spirit of God lives in you. And if anyone does not have the Spirit of Christ, they do not belong to Christ. ¹⁰But if Christ is in you, then even though your body is subject to death because of sin, the Spirit gives life because of righteousness. ¹¹And if the Spirit of him who raised Jesus from the dead is living in you, he who raised Christ from the dead will also give life to your mortal bodies because of his Spirit who lives in you **(Romans 8:5-11,** TNIV).

The key words are "mind set," and "control." Mindset refers directly to thinking. Control refers to our submission. Regarding our sinful nature (we all have one), if our minds are set on this; we are thinking bottom-up. If our minds are set on the Spirit (God's Holy Spirit) we are thinking top-down. Bottom-up thinking produces death (all things which bring forth no life, nothing eternal)! Top-down thinking produces LIFE AND PEACE! The sinful mind (bottom-up) is hostile to God and cannot please him: *⁷The sinful mind is hostile to God; it does not submit to God's law, nor can it do so. ⁸Those controlled by the sinful nature cannot please God.* **But those controlled by God's Spirit (top-down) are alive with God's very life!** Verse **11** is very important: *And if the Spirit of him who raised Jesus from the dead is living in you, he who raised Christ from the dead will also give life to your mortal bodies because of his Spirit who lives in you.* Mortal bodies, ALIVE, because of God's resident Spirit and our top-down thinking, refers to our behavior. How shall we conduct ourselves in this world? We shall be obedient to our Lord. Alive to his thoughts, alive to his will and purpose. Alive to accomplish his purpose (our behavior). Alive to his glory.

We are free. Free to think bottom-up as slaves or free to think top-down seeing God at work. Free to join him at his work. Free to listen and hear his purpose for us. Free to fulfill our specific purpose in God's kingdom. Free to behave in such a way as to bring him praise and honor and glory. Free to enjoy him forever!

What are you thinking?

QUESTIONS TO PROVOKE CHANGE

1. Explain the "shackles" of bottom-up thinking (Ephesians 4:17-19).

2. Explain freedom to think top-down (Ephesians 4:20-24).

3. When we are "free" to think top-down, why would we continue to think bottom-up? (Galatians 5:1)

4. Explain the "mindset" and "control" themes in Romans 8:5-11. How does this impact top-down thinking? What do we have to do to begin to think top-down?

Notes and Thoughts:

F. Michael Grubbs

CHAPTER 8
WORRY-LESS

Fretting, disquiet, anxiousness and many more forms of worry are hindrances to a productive Christian life. Everyone who breathes experiences these emotions, some more than others. Worry involves the immediate and the future. Rarely, does one worry about the past because it is fixed, static, unchangeable. But the immediate and future are yet to be and largely out of our control. So, we worry. We also have the fortunate and unfortunate gift of imagination. Fortunate, because it can perceive all kinds of good; unfortunate, because it can foresee terrible possible things. Good and terrible are also tricky concepts. Think of Joseph; sold into slavery to Egypt by his brothers, jailed, then raised to authority; separated from his family and people. Some might say that was terrible. Listen to Joseph's top-down assessment, speaking to his brothers:

> *You intended to harm me, but God intended it all for good. He brought me to this position so I could save the lives of many people* **(Genesis 50:20,** NLT**).**

Now Joseph's brothers were very worried because this powerful man, their brother, whom they had severely wronged, now had them in his custody to do with them as he pleased. **Fear promotes bottom-up thinking.** Pay attention to the next verse:

No, don't be afraid. I will continue to take care of you and your children." So he reassured them by speaking kindly to them **(Genesis 50:21,** NLT**).**

I am sure the brothers felt great relief, perhaps they began to understand that God is in control. Much worry and consternation can be avoided by thinking from God's point of view, even when it looks like the worst is about to happen.

Jesus had some things to say about worry. I am sure you are familiar with these words:

Can all your worries add a single moment to your life? [26] *And if worry can't accomplish a little thing like that, what's the use of worrying over bigger things?* [27] *"Look at the lilies and how they grow. They don't work or make their clothing, yet Solomon in all his glory was not dressed as beautifully as they are.* [28] *And if God cares so wonderfully for flowers that are here today and thrown into the fire tomorrow, he will certainly care for you. Why do you have so little faith?* [29] *"And don't be concerned about what to eat and what to drink. Don't worry about such things.* [30] *These things dominate the thoughts of unbelievers all over the world, but your Father already knows your needs.* [31] *Seek the Kingdom of God above all else, and he will give you everything you need.* [32] *"So don't be afraid, little flock. For it gives your Father great happiness to give you the Kingdom.* [33] *"Sell your possessions and give to those in need. This will store up treasure for you in heaven! And the purses of heaven never get old or develop holes. Your treasure will be safe; no thief can steal it and no moth can destroy it.* [34] *Wherever your treasure is, there the desires of your heart will also be* **(Luke 12:25-34,** NLT**).**

Jesus encountered a culture of bottom-up thinkers. Worry was a part of everyday life for them. Things have not changed in two thousand years: can you add even a minute to your life by worrying? Worry is a part of everyday life for our culture, too. It is all bottom-up thinking. Jesus is introducing his listeners (and us) to top-down thinking in these verses. First, he says worry is non-productive, futile (*what's the use of worrying?*). Life's worries are manifold, in fact there is no end to them. Jesus mentions eating, drinking, clothing; he could have mentioned health, work, driving, debt, housing, marrying, children, accident, etc. you get the idea. Worry comes from bottom-up thinking and creates a stagnation of top-down behavior. This is thinking that does not consider an all-knowing, all-powerful God who loves you. It is bottom-up and a trap! Then Jesus speaks about birds and flowers. Surely, he cares for birds and flowers; but how much more does he care for you? *These things dominate the thoughts of unbelievers all over the world, but your Father already knows your needs*. The unbelievers (bottom-up thinkers) allow their thoughts to be dominated by the seeking of common needs. The Greek word for our translation "dominated" literally means: *search (inquire) for; to demand, to crave*:—desire, enquire, seek (after, for)[4]. In other words, to strive for, or to worry about. Jesus then introduces the all-knowing Father. **He knows what you need!** When we dare to think top-down worry becomes a fly buzzing around; irritating but unimportant. When we dare to think and believe top-down worry disappears. It is replaced with eager anticipation to see what God will do next!

> *You will keep in perfect peace those whose minds are steadfast, because they trust in you. ⁴Trust in the LORD forever, for the LORD, the LORD, is the Rock eternal* **(Isaiah 26:3-4, TNIV)**.

Please read these verses several times. "You," the first word, refers to God. God will keep in perfect peace the mind that steadfastly trusts God! **This is top-down thinking!** Worry (bottom-up thinking) is a destroyer of peace. The mind operating from top-down is KEPT in perfect peace by God because of our trust. Verse 4 then describes who we trust; the LORD, the Rock eternal! JESUS!

At the last supper Jesus was with his disciples. John records his last teachings beginning with Chapter 14. He has just washed their feet (Chapter 13) and now teaches them about his suffering, death, and resurrection. They are thinking bottom-up. They are worried. Listen to his words to them:

> *Peace I leave with you; my peace I give you. I do not give to you as the world gives. Do not let your hearts be troubled and do not be afraid* **(John 14:27, TNIV)**.

What kind of peace does he give them (us)? MY PEACE I GIVE YOU! Not the shallow, powerless peace that the world gives. Jesus is heading for the cross, quite possibly the cruelest death ever devised. The world would have him hiding and cringing, but he is giving his peace away! Because he thinks top-down he knows peace. Because he trusts his Father he knows peace. When we think top-down we will know peace. We will have his peace. At the end of this last teaching, just before Jesus goes to the garden of Gethsemane to pray, Jesus says:

> *I have told you these things, so that in me you may have peace. In this world you will have trouble. But take heart! I have overcome the world"* **(John 16:33, TNIV)**.

Jesus is saying that in him (top-down thinking) we can have peace. While we are alive in this world, we will have trouble. Jesus' overcoming of the world enables us to think and behave in positive ways even in the midst of grave difficulty.

In her book, *Fantastic Beasts and Where to Find Them* J.K. Rowling created a character called Newt Scamander; here is a quote taken from that book. Newt Scamander: "My philosophy is that **worrying** means you suffer twice." What Rowling is conveying, through Newt, is that bottom-up thinking leads us to suffer what **might** happen, then if the worst happens we suffer again. When we think top-down, from God's perspective we know that even suffering brings about his good will.

> *And the God of all grace, who called you to his eternal glory in Christ, after you have suffered a little while, will himself restore you and make you strong, firm and steadfast. ¹¹To him be the power for ever and ever. Amen* **(1 Peter 5:10-11,** TNIV**)**.

God is gracious; he invites you to eternal glory in Christ! Compared to the promise of eternal glory (top-down thinking); what is suffering? We do not like it, do not desire it; but compared with eternal glory we can endure it. We can let suffering do its work in us.

> *For our present troubles are small and won't last very long. Yet they produce for us a glory that vastly outweighs them and will last forever! 18 So we don't look at the troubles we can see now; rather, we fix our gaze on things that cannot be seen. For the things we see now will soon be gone, but the things we cannot see will last forever* **(2 Corinthians 4:17-18,** TNIV**)**.

This is top-down thinking. Focusing on what we cannot see with our eyes, but can see with our spirits, our Almighty God and his Kingdom. Worrying; why would you want to suffer twice? One more Scripture related to worry versus top-down thinking:

> *"But blessed are those who trust in the LORD, whose confidence is in him. ⁸They will be like a tree planted by the water that sends out its roots by the stream. It does not fear when heat comes; its leaves are always green. It has no worries in a year of drought and never fails to bear fruit." ⁹The heart is deceitful above all things and beyond cure. Who can understand it?*
> *¹⁰"I the LORD search the heart and examine the mind, to reward everyone according to their conduct, according to what their deeds deserve"* **(Jeremiah 17:7-10,** TNIV**)**.

The prophet Jeremiah, speaking for God, uses a metaphor. He is saying that those who trust in the Lord, whose hope and confidence are in God (top-down thinking) are like a tree planted by a river with roots reaching deep into the water. Heat and drought do not bother or worry this tree. It never fails to produce fruit. **This is what top-down thinking does for the believer**. It enables the Christ-follower to behave according to God's direction. Jeremiah goes on to say that bottom-up thinking and the heart that is more deceitfully wicked than all else are known by God. Both the mind and the heart are known by God! Therefore, God renews the mind to think from his perspective and not our own and he transforms the hard heart of the unbeliever into the heart on fire for God! When we think top-down his examination of our behavior ends in reward and our actions are deserving of praise. "Well done, good and faithful servant." Top-down thinking makes us worry-less.

QUESTIONS TO PROVOKE CHANGE

1. Top-down thinking enables us to overcome worry, how?

2. Top-down thinking enables us to overcome fear, how?

3. "When we dare to think top-down worry becomes a fly buzzing around; irritating but unimportant. When we dare to think, and believe top-down worry disappears." Discuss the importance of these two sentences to you.

4. Isaiah 26:3-4 is an important top-down passage; discuss how it affects you?

5. Discuss the two "peace" verses in John 14 and John 16. How do these promote assurance?

6. How does "fixing our eyes on what is unseen" imply top-down thinking?

7. Explain top-down thinking in Jeremiah 17:7-10.

Notes and Thoughts:

CHAPTER 9
CONFIDENCE: STRONG AND COURAGEOUS

Have I not commanded you? Be strong and courageous. Do not be afraid; do not be discouraged, for the LORD your God will be with you wherever you go" **(Joshua 1:9, TNIV)**.

God spoke these words to Joshua as he became Israel's leader after Moses died. He was about to lead Israel across the Jordan river and into the promised land. Four times God said to Joshua; "Be strong and courageous." Why? Because he was not strong and courageous! I can only imagine Joshua looking out over a million people and all their livestock piled up along the banks of the Jordan river, at flood stage, getting ready to cross into a land filled with hostile people. He might have been thinking bottom-up, even though his whole life he had seen God do miracle after miracle. Now he was the leader. God speaks to him four times and Joshua begins to think top-down. Hearing God's encouragement fills him with the strength and courage to boldly trust his God. You should read the rest of the book of Joshua to see what happens. It is quite exciting. God's promises prove faithful as they always do. In this chapter, we will lightly review the first two parts of this book and conclude with the challenges laid before us by the same God; Joshua's faithful, all-powerful God, the only God, our God.

In Part 1 of this book we discovered that it is God who gives us identity. We begin to live in this identity when we begin to see ourselves as he sees us (top-down). We are loved so deeply it is beyond our reckoning.

> *Then Christ will make his home in your hearts as you trust in him. Your roots will grow down into God's love and keep you strong. [18] And may you have the power to understand, as all God's people should, how wide, how long, how high, and how deep his love is. [19] May you experience the love of Christ, though it is too great to understand fully. Then you will be made complete with all the fullness of life and power that comes from God* **(Ephesians 3:17-19,** NLT).

As you trust Jesus, he dwells in the deepest parts of you. The very roots of your soul, your thinking included, grows strong in God's love. *And may you have the power to understand*; this is directly related to top-down thinking. Power to understand the enormity of God's love for you. This is your identity! This love is so enormous that we cannot fully comprehend it. It goes on and on and on ... *Then you will be made complete with all the fullness of life and power that comes from God.* You could spend the rest of your time on earth contemplating the meaning of these words in this passage. Suffice it to say; our complete and true identity comes from thinking about ourselves as God sees us! In him we lack nothing. This top-down thinking gives us great confidence.

> *What shall we say about such wonderful things as these? If God is for us, who can ever be against us?*
> **(Romans 8:31,** NLT).

There are many things against us, but they all come to nothing, because God is for us! Be strong and courageous.

In Part 2 of this book you learned that God has purpose for you. **You are significant**. We learned that when he transforms us from bottom-up thinkers and renews our minds to be top-down thinkers he reveals his will, his purpose for you.

> *Don't copy the behavior and customs of this world, but let God transform you into a new person by changing the way you think. Then you will learn to know God's will for you, which is good and pleasing and perfect* **(Romans 12:2, NLT)**.

By practicing listening to God, in the chair, he clarifies this purpose and we can then set out to obey him. Listen to the concluding verse of the above Ephesians passage:

> *Now all glory to God, who is able, through his mighty power at work within us, to accomplish infinitely more than we might ask or think.* **(Ephesians 3:20,** NLT**)**.

God's mighty power is at work in you!

As we think top-down, as we think his thoughts; we are able to accomplish infinitely more than what we might ask or imagine.' What **we** might ask or imagine is bottom-up! Top-down thinking, according to his plan, will enable us to accomplish infinitely more because his power is at work **in us**!

This chapter is about thinking top-down regarding our confidence to accomplish what God desires, what God has planned for you. Consider this passage:

> *Remember, dear brothers and sisters, that few of you were wise in the world's eyes or powerful or wealthy when God called you. [27] Instead, God chose things the world considers foolish in order to shame those who think they are wise. And he chose things that are powerless to shame those who are powerful. [28] God chose things despised by the world, things counted as nothing at all, and used them to bring to nothing what the world considers important. [29] As a result, no one can ever boast in the presence of God. [30] God has united you with Christ Jesus. For our benefit God made him to be wisdom itself. Christ made us right*

with God; he made us pure and holy, and he freed us from sin. ³¹ Therefore, as the Scriptures say, "If you want to boast, boast only about the LORD" **(1 Corinthians 1:26-31,** NLT**).**

God does not start with hall-of-famers, PhD's, the bright and beautiful or the powerfully rich. Those who are highly elevated by society. That is where we would begin, when we used to think bottom-up. **Rather, he chooses you and me!** What he is going to do with us is 'shame the wise;' meaning top-down thinking puts to shame bottom-up thinking: 'shame the strong;' meaning top-down obedience wins the day. In the end top-down thinking will 'bring to nothing' all bottom-up thinking so: NO ONE CAN BOAST BEFORE THE LORD! It is all because of Jesus: our righteousness, our holiness, our redemption that we can boast IN the Lord. This is our confidence! Be strong and courageous.

When they saw the courage of Peter and John and realized that they were unschooled, ordinary men, they were astonished and they took note that these men had been with Jesus. ¹⁴But since they could see the man who had been healed standing there with them, there was nothing they could say. ¹⁵So they ordered them to withdraw from the Sanhedrin and then conferred together. ¹⁶"What are we going to do with these men?" they asked. "Everyone living in Jerusalem knows they have performed a notable sign, and we cannot deny it. ¹⁷But to stop this thing from spreading any further among the people, we must warn them to speak no longer to anyone in this name."¹⁸Then they called them in again and commanded them not to speak or teach at all in the name of Jesus. ¹⁹But Peter and John replied, "Which is right in God's eyes: to listen to you, or to him? You be the judges! ²⁰As for us, we cannot help speaking about what we have seen and heard" **(Acts 4:13-20,** TNIV**).**

Peter and John had just acted in Jesus' name (top-down) and a lame man was healed. He was lame from birth and was now more than forty years old. This upset the bottom-up thinkers terribly. They hauled Peter and John off to be rebuked by the authorities who told them not to speak in Jesus' name. Take note of what the bottom-up thinkers saw in Peter and John. *When they saw the courage of Peter and John and realized that they were unschooled, ordinary men, they were astonished and they took note that these men had been with Jesus.* They saw courage and confidence! There was no fear in Peter and John, though they were ordinary and uneducated, they were transformed by the renewing of their minds. They took note that Peter and John had been with Jesus! YES! Peter and John were top-down thinkers! Strong and courageous! They knew what the Master desired of them and they insisted on doing it. *As for us, we cannot help speaking about what we have seen and heard."*

God uses ordinary, unschooled people. This does not mean that we should remain ordinary or unschooled. No Christ-follower would call Peter and John ordinary or unschooled today. They wrote 7 books of the New Testament between them! They were founders and leaders of the Church in Jerusalem! But to the bottom-up thinkers they were ordinary fishermen, uneducated men. **God saw them through his eyes, they began to see themselves through God's eyes.** They began to think top-down and God's purposes were accomplished mightily through them, beyond what they could have asked or imagined. God wants you to have the same experience of transformation; to be used by him mightily. Paul wrote some amazing words to the church at Rome, a fledgling church at the time; a church with no theologians.

> *I myself am convinced, my brothers and sisters, that you yourselves are full of goodness, filled with knowledge and competent to instruct one another* **(Romans 15:14,** TNIV**)**.

Full of goodness because Jesus fills you with his Holy Spirit. Filled with knowledge because you think top-down, competent to instruct because you begin to speak his words, not your own.

Let's review:

And we have received God's Spirit (not the world's spirit), so we can know the wonderful things God has freely given us. ¹³When we tell you these things, we do not use words that come from human wisdom. Instead, we speak words given to us by the Spirit, using the Spirit's words to explain spiritual truths **(1 Corinthians 2:12-13, TNIV)**.

This is CONFIDENT, TOP-DOWN THINKING. It is for you. Be strong and courageous.

Some last comments

Rejoice in the Lord always. I will say it again: Rejoice! ⁵Let your gentleness be evident to all. The Lord is near. ⁶Do not be anxious about anything, but in every situation, by prayer and petition, with thanksgiving, present your requests to God. ⁷And the peace of God, which transcends all understanding, will guard your hearts and your minds in Christ Jesus **(Philippians 4:4-7, TNIV)**.

Our joy in the Lord Jesus should always be overflowing into the lives of others because he is always with us. This deletes anxiety (worry-less). We should be praying prayers of thanksgiving, listening for his orders, and be quick to obey. The result is that God's peace becomes our peace. This peace transcends all bottom-up thinking. It guards our hearts and minds (by top-down thinking) in Jesus Christ.

In the parable of the Master who took a trip, **Matthew 25:14-30**, the servant who was given the most did the most with what he was given. LET THIS BE YOU! Pay attention to his reward:

"His master replied, 'Well done, good and faithful servant! You have been faithful with a few things; I will put you in charge of many things. Come and share your master's happiness!' **(Matthew 25:23, TNIV)**.

BE STRONG AND COURAGEOUS! SHARE IN THE MASTER'S HAPPINESS!

THINK TOP-DOWN!

QUESTIONS TO PROVOKE CHANGE

1. Explain Joshua's conversion to top-down thinking. Who helped him do it? Who will help you do it, if you ask him?

2. In Ephesians 3:17-19 God's love is described; discuss this. Discuss verse 19 regarding top-down thinking.

3. Explain Ephesians 3:20 in the light of bottom-up thinking.

4. God's glory is demonstrated when he uses ordinary people to do extraordinary things (1 Corinthians 1:26-31). How does this make you feel? What can you anticipate when you think top-down?

5. Peter and John were strong and courageous (Acts 4:13-20). Because of top-down thinking you too can be strong and courageous. Discuss how you feel about this.

Notes and Thoughts:

ENDNOTES

1 James Strong, A Concise Dictionary of the Words in the Greek Testament and The Hebrew Bible (Bellingham, WA: Logos Bible Software, 2009), 25.

2 Inc Merriam-Webster, Merriam-Webster's Collegiate Dictionary. (Springfield, MA: Merriam-Webster, Inc., 2003).

3 Johannes P. Louw and Eugene Albert Nida, Greek-English Lexicon of the New Testament: Based on Semantic Domains (New York: United Bible Societies, 1996), 769.

4 James Strong, A Concise Dictionary of the Words in the Greek Testament and The Hebrew Bible (Bellingham, WA: Logos Bible Software, 2009), 31.

ABOUT THE AUTHOR

Dr. F. Michael Grubbs is the Christian Counselor and Coach at The Lyndon Center in Kansas City. With over 35 years in pastoral ministry, he has encouraged many in their walk towards freedom and the abundant life Jesus Christ offers. He holds a MS in Christian Counseling from Cairn University; Langhorne, PA and a Doctor of Counseling from Midwestern Baptist Theological Seminary, Kansas City, MO.

ADDITIONAL READING BY F. MICHAEL GRUBBS

Broken Chains: Freedom from Unwanted Habits and Addictions
Broken Chains describes the cause, remedy, and maintenance of liberty from habits and addictions. The book is based on biblical truth applied in individual reality. Part One describes the nature of addictiveness and its cause. Part Two describes how one can be freed from the habit or addiction. Part Three describes how one remains free. The book is designed to be read by an individual as well as with two or more people. End of chapter questions assist in facilitating group discussions. The book is available at amazon.com in both paperback and eBook versions.

ABOUT THE LYNDON CENTER

The purpose of The Lyndon Center is to offer Christian counseling and coaching which integrates biblical truths. The goal is to aid each person served to achieve healthy emotional and spiritual potential within the context of Christian principles. More information is available at www.thelyndoncenter.com.

Made in the USA
Coppell, TX
07 November 2021